Lady Bird Johnson and the Natic

American

Address Book

Abbeville Press · Publishers

National Wildflower Research Center

The National Wildflower Research Center, a nonprofit organization, was established in 1982 to stimulate and carry out research on conservation and cultivation of wildflowers and native plants, in cooperation with universities, botanic gardens, arboreta, and other institutions throughout North America. Through these efforts the Center aims to reestablish native plants in landscapes, thereby aiding in the repair and beautification of the environment.

The Wildflower Center also collects information on why, when, where, and how to establish wildflower plantings and native plant landscapes, and through its Clearinghouse provides this information to the public. The Center also has a national membership program; dues start at $25. Membership benefits include newsletters, journals, seminars, conferences, tours, and other benefits in addition to free Clearinghouse information. For more information, write Membership, National Wildflower Research Center, 2600 FM 973 North, Austin, Texas 78725, or call (512) 929-3600. To ask for Clearinghouse information for your area, send a self-addressed mailing label plus $4 for postage and handling to "Clearinghouse" at the address above.

Cover: PINK MONKEYFLOWERS, LUPINE, ASTERS, AND QUEEN ANNE'S LACE (Mimulus lewisii, Lupinus perennis, Aster laevis, Daucus carota), Washington. Photograph by Pat O'Hara.

Previous page: Columbine (Aquilegia sp.), Oregon. Photograph by Steve Terrill.

Commentaries by Beth Anderson, Resource Botanist, National Wildflower Research Center, Austin, Texas.

OCOTILLO (Fouquieria splendens), Texas.
Photograph by David Muench.

For most of the year, the spiny stems of ocotillo look dry and leafless. With the coming of spring rains, however, the stems turn green with a mass of tiny leaves, terminating in brilliant clusters of red flowers. Shown here in the Chihuahuan Desert, ocotillo grows on rocky hillsides from Texas to California and south to Mexico.

SEEP-SPRING MONKEYFLOWERS (Mimulus guttatus), Washington.
Photograph by Steve Terrill.

*Seep-spring monkeyflowers thrive in seeps, springs, ditches, and along streams at lower to mid-mountain elevations in the Northwest. The species name (**guttatus**), which means spotted or speckled, refers to the dotted lower lip of the flower. Seep-spring monkeyflowers bloom from May to September.*

Name _____ *Phone* _____

Address _____

City & State _____ *Zip* _____ *Birthday* _____

Name _____ *Phone* _____

Address _____

City & State _____ *Zip* _____ *Birthday* _____

Name _____ *Phone* _____

Address _____

City & State _____ *Zip* _____ *Birthday* _____

Name _____ *Phone* _____

Address _____

City & State _____ *Zip* _____ *Birthday* _____

Name _____ *Phone* _____

Address _____

City & State _____ *Zip* _____ *Birthday* _____

Name _____ *Phone* _____

Address _____

City & State _____ *Zip* _____ *Birthday* _____

Name _____ *Phone* _____

Address _____

City & State _____ *Zip* _____ *Birthday* _____

Name _____ *Phone* _____

Address _____

City & State _____ *Zip* _____ *Birthday* _____

Name		*Phone*
Address		
City & State	*Zip*	*Birthday*

Name		*Phone*
Address		
City & State	*Zip*	*Birthday*

Name		*Phone*
Address		
City & State	*Zip*	*Birthday*

Name		*Phone*
Address		
City & State	*Zip*	*Birthday*

Name		*Phone*
Address		
City & State	*Zip*	*Birthday*

Name		*Phone*
Address		
City & State	*Zip*	*Birthday*

Name		*Phone*
Address		
City & State	*Zip*	*Birthday*

Name		*Phone*
Address		
City & State	*Zip*	*Birthday*

Name _____ *Phone* _____

Address _____

City & State _____ *Zip* _____ *Birthday* _____

Name _____ *Phone* _____

Address _____

City & State _____ *Zip* _____ *Birthday* _____

Name _____ *Phone* _____

Address _____

City & State _____ *Zip* _____ *Birthday* _____

Name _____ *Phone* _____

Address _____

City & State _____ *Zip* _____ *Birthday* _____

Name _____ *Phone* _____

Address _____

City & State _____ *Zip* _____ *Birthday* _____

Name _____ *Phone* _____

Address _____

City & State _____ *Zip* _____ *Birthday* _____

Name _____ *Phone* _____

Address _____

City & State _____ *Zip* _____ *Birthday* _____

Name _____ *Phone* _____

Address _____

City & State _____ *Zip* _____ *Birthday* _____

Name	Phone
Address	
City & State Zip	Birthday

Name	Phone
Address	
City & State Zip	Birthday

Name	Phone
Address	
City & State Zip	Birthday

Name	Phone
Address	
City & State Zip	Birthday

Name	Phone
Address	
City & State Zip	Birthday

Name	Phone
Address	
City & State Zip	Birthday

Name	Phone
Address	
City & State Zip	Birthday

Name	Phone
Address	
City & State Zip	Birthday

SHOWY LADY'S SLIPPER (Cypripedium reginae), Michigan.
Photograph by Rod Planck.

One of the loveliest native orchids, showy lady's slipper grows in acidic soils of bogs and damp woods, and ranges from Newfoundland to Manitoba and south to the eastern United States. The flowers bloom from May to August. Like many orchids, showy lady's slipper is becoming rare due to loss of habitat and overcollection.

NORTHERN DOWNY VIOLET *(Viola fimbriatula)*, *Michigan.*
Photograph by John Shaw.

One of the many members of the violet family, northern downy violet is a small plant with arrowhead-shaped leaves. It grows in dry woods and open slopes from Nova Scotia to Minnesota, south to Florida, California, and Oklahoma. Blooms appear in the spring.

Name		*Phone*
Address		
City & State	*Zip*	*Birthday*

Name		*Phone*
Address		
City & State	*Zip*	*Birthday*

Name		*Phone*
Address		
City & State	*Zip*	*Birthday*

Name		*Phone*
Address		
City & State	*Zip*	*Birthday*

Name		*Phone*
Address		
City & State	*Zip*	*Birthday*

Name		*Phone*
Address		
City & State	*Zip*	*Birthday*

Name		*Phone*
Address		
City & State	*Zip*	*Birthday*

Name		*Phone*
Address		
City & State	*Zip*	*Birthday*

Name _____ *Phone* _____

Address _____

City & State _____ *Zip* ____ *Birthday* _____

Name _____ *Phone* _____

Address _____

City & State _____ *Zip* ____ *Birthday* _____

Name _____ *Phone* _____

Address _____

City & State _____ *Zip* ____ *Birthday* _____

Name _____ *Phone* _____

Address _____

City & State _____ *Zip* ____ *Birthday* _____

Name _____ *Phone* _____

Address _____

City & State _____ *Zip* ____ *Birthday* _____

Name _____ *Phone* _____

Address _____

City & State _____ *Zip* ____ *Birthday* _____

Name _____ *Phone* _____

Address _____

City & State _____ *Zip* ____ *Birthday* _____

Name _____ *Phone* _____

Address _____

City & State _____ *Zip* ____ *Birthday* _____

Name _____   *Phone* _____

Address _____

City & State _____ *Zip* _____   *Birthday* _____

Name _____   *Phone* _____

Address _____

City & State _____ *Zip* _____   *Birthday* _____

Name _____   *Phone* _____

Address _____

City & State _____ *Zip* _____   *Birthday* _____

Name _____   *Phone* _____

Address _____

City & State _____ *Zip* _____   *Birthday* _____

Name _____   *Phone* _____

Address _____

City & State _____ *Zip* _____   *Birthday* _____

Name _____   *Phone* _____

Address _____

City & State _____ *Zip* _____   *Birthday* _____

Name _____   *Phone* _____

Address _____

City & State _____ *Zip* _____   *Birthday* _____

Name _____   *Phone* _____

Address _____

City & State _____ *Zip* _____   *Birthday* _____

Name		Phone	
Address			
City & State	Zip	Birthday	

Name		Phone	
Address			
City & State	Zip	Birthday	

Name		Phone	
Address			
City & State	Zip	Birthday	

Name		Phone	
Address			
City & State	Zip	Birthday	

Name		Phone	
Address			
City & State	Zip	Birthday	

Name		Phone	
Address			
City & State	Zip	Birthday	

Name		Phone	
Address			
City & State	Zip	Birthday	

Name		Phone	
Address			
City & State	Zip	Birthday	

*LOMATIUM (**Lomatium** sp.), Oregon.*
Photograph by Steve Terrill.

Over thirty species of **Lomatium** occur throughout much of the Pacific Northwest. Members of the carrot family, those species prefer dry, rocky soils. The flowers—arranged in compound umbels—bloom from spring to summer. The genus name comes from the Greek word **loma**, which means "a border," and refers to the winged or ribbed fruit.

CLARET CUP CACTUS (Echinocereus triglochidiatus), Texas.
Photograph by David Muench.

Claret cup cactus prefers dry, rocky, or sandy hills, ledges, and canyons, and ranges from southeastern California, east to Texas, and north to southern Utah and Colorado. Like many cacti, claret cup grows in clumps, sometimes forming large, cushionlike mounds. Masses of crimson flowers bloom in early spring, from April to May.

C

Name _____ Phone _____

Address _____

City & State _____ Zip _____ Birthday _____

Name _____ Phone _____

Address _____

City & State _____ Zip _____ Birthday _____

Name _____ Phone _____

Address _____

City & State _____ Zip _____ Birthday _____

Name _____ Phone _____

Address _____

City & State _____ Zip _____ Birthday _____

Name _____ Phone _____

Address _____

City & State _____ Zip _____ Birthday _____

Name _____ Phone _____

Address _____

City & State _____ Zip _____ Birthday _____

Name _____ Phone _____

Address _____

City & State _____ Zip _____ Birthday _____

Name _____ Phone _____

Address _____

City & State _____ Zip _____ Birthday _____

Name		*Phone*
Address		
City & State	*Zip*	*Birthday*

Name		*Phone*
Address		
City & State	*Zip*	*Birthday*

Name		*Phone*
Address		
City & State	*Zip*	*Birthday*

Name		*Phone*
Address		
City & State	*Zip*	*Birthday*

Name		*Phone*
Address		
City & State	*Zip*	*Birthday*

Name		*Phone*
Address		
City & State	*Zip*	*Birthday*

Name		*Phone*
Address		
City & State	*Zip*	*Birthday*

Name		*Phone*
Address		
City & State	*Zip*	*Birthday*

Name _____ *Phone* _____

Address _____

City & State _____ *Zip* _____ *Birthday* _____

Name _____ *Phone* _____

Address _____

City & State _____ *Zip* _____ *Birthday* _____

Name _____ *Phone* _____

Address _____

City & State _____ *Zip* _____ *Birthday* _____

Name _____ *Phone* _____

Address _____

City & State _____ *Zip* _____ *Birthday* _____

Name _____ *Phone* _____

Address _____

City & State _____ *Zip* _____ *Birthday* _____

Name _____ *Phone* _____

Address _____

City & State _____ *Zip* _____ *Birthday* _____

Name _____ *Phone* _____

Address _____

City & State _____ *Zip* _____ *Birthday* _____

Name _____ *Phone* _____

Address _____

City & State _____ *Zip* _____ *Birthday* _____

Name _____ *Phone* _____

Address _____

City & State _____ *Zip* _____ *Birthday* _____

Name _____ *Phone* _____

Address _____

City & State _____ *Zip* _____ *Birthday* _____

Name _____ *Phone* _____

Address _____

City & State _____ *Zip* _____ *Birthday* _____

Name _____ *Phone* _____

Address _____

City & State _____ *Zip* _____ *Birthday* _____

Name _____ *Phone* _____

Address _____

City & State _____ *Zip* _____ *Birthday* _____

Name _____ *Phone* _____

Address _____

City & State _____ *Zip* _____ *Birthday* _____

Name _____ *Phone* _____

Address _____

City & State _____ *Zip* _____ *Birthday* _____

Name _____ *Phone* _____

Address _____

City & State _____ *Zip* _____ *Birthday* _____

LUPINES (**Lupinus** *sp.*), *Minnesota.*
Photograph by Mike Magnuson.

A member of the legume family, the genus **Lupinus** *includes some 200 species worldwide.* **Lupinus**
comes from the Latin word **lupus**, *for wolf. Since lupines often grow successfully in poor soils, at one
time they were thought to devour soil nutrients as a wolf devours its prey. Lupines vary in color from
white to pink to deep purple or blue and range widely throughout North America.*

COLUMBIAN LILY (Lilium columbianum), Washington.
Photograph by Pat O'Hara.

One of the many lily species found in the Pacific Northwest, Columbian lily grows in damp woods and open meadows from northwest California to British Columbia and west to the Great Basin. The showy blossoms appear from June to July.

D

Name		*Phone*
Address		
City & State	*Zip*	*Birthday*

Name		*Phone*
Address		
City & State	*Zip*	*Birthday*

Name		*Phone*
Address		
City & State	*Zip*	*Birthday*

Name		*Phone*
Address		
City & State	*Zip*	*Birthday*

Name		*Phone*
Address		
City & State	*Zip*	*Birthday*

Name		*Phone*
Address		
City & State	*Zip*	*Birthday*

Name		*Phone*
Address		
City & State	*Zip*	*Birthday*

Name		*Phone*
Address		
City & State	*Zip*	*Birthday*

Name		Phone
Address		
City & State	Zip	Birthday

Name		Phone
Address		
City & State	Zip	Birthday

Name		Phone
Address		
City & State	Zip	Birthday

Name		Phone
Address		
City & State	Zip	Birthday

Name		Phone
Address		
City & State	Zip	Birthday

Name		Phone
Address		
City & State	Zip	Birthday

Name		Phone
Address		
City & State	Zip	Birthday

Name		Phone
Address		
City & State	Zip	Birthday

Name		_Phone_
Address		
City & State	_Zip_	_Birthday_

Name		_Phone_
Address		
City & State	_Zip_	_Birthday_

Name		_Phone_
Address		
City & State	_Zip_	_Birthday_

Name		_Phone_
Address		
City & State	_Zip_	_Birthday_

Name		_Phone_
Address		
City & State	_Zip_	_Birthday_

Name		_Phone_
Address		
City & State	_Zip_	_Birthday_

Name		_Phone_
Address		
City & State	_Zip_	_Birthday_

Name		_Phone_
Address		
City & State	_Zip_	_Birthday_

Name _____ *Phone* _____

Address _____

City & State _____ *Zip* _____ *Birthday* _____

Name _____ *Phone* _____

Address _____

City & State _____ *Zip* _____ *Birthday* _____

Name _____ *Phone* _____

Address _____

City & State _____ *Zip* _____ *Birthday* _____

Name _____ *Phone* _____

Address _____

City & State _____ *Zip* _____ *Birthday* _____

Name _____ *Phone* _____

Address _____

City & State _____ *Zip* _____ *Birthday* _____

Name _____ *Phone* _____

Address _____

City & State _____ *Zip* _____ *Birthday* _____

Name _____ *Phone* _____

Address _____

City & State _____ *Zip* _____ *Birthday* _____

Name _____ *Phone* _____

Address _____

City & State _____ *Zip* _____ *Birthday* _____

PINK MOUNTAIN HEATHER (Phyllodoce empetriformis), Washington.
Photograph by Pat O'Hara.

This small evergreen shrub is found at high altitudes on moist to wet soils from a little below timberline to well above it. The species ranges from Alaska to Alberta and south to California and Colorado, and blooms from the end of June to the beginning of August. Phyllodoce was a sea nymph in ancient Greek mythology.

DUNE PRIMROSE (Oenothera sp.), California.
Photograph by David Muench.

Highly drought-tolerant, many **Oenothera** species grow in dry, sandy, desert soils of the Southwest.
The fragrant white or light-colored flowers, which bloom from spring to summer, are pollinated at night
by moths.

Name _____ *Phone* _____

Address _____

City & State _____ *Zip* _____ *Birthday* _____

Name _____ *Phone* _____

Address _____

City & State _____ *Zip* _____ *Birthday* _____

E
F

Name _____ *Phone* _____

Address _____

City & State _____ *Zip* _____ *Birthday* _____

Name _____ *Phone* _____

Address _____

City & State _____ *Zip* _____ *Birthday* _____

Name _____ *Phone* _____

Address _____

City & State _____ *Zip* _____ *Birthday* _____

Name _____ *Phone* _____

Address _____

City & State _____ *Zip* _____ *Birthday* _____

Name _____ *Phone* _____

Address _____

City & State _____ *Zip* _____ *Birthday* _____

Name _____   *Phone* _____

Address _____

City & State _____ *Zip* _____   *Birthday* _____

Name _____   *Phone* _____

Address _____

City & State _____ *Zip* _____   *Birthday* _____

Name _____   *Phone* _____

Address _____

City & State _____ *Zip* _____   *Birthday* _____

Name _____   *Phone* _____

Address _____

City & State _____ *Zip* _____   *Birthday* _____

Name _____   *Phone* _____

Address _____

City & State _____ *Zip* _____   *Birthday* _____

Name _____   *Phone* _____

Address _____

City & State _____ *Zip* _____   *Birthday* _____

Name _____   *Phone* _____

Address _____

City & State _____ *Zip* _____   *Birthday* _____

Name _____   *Phone* _____

Address _____

City & State _____ *Zip* _____   *Birthday* _____

Name		*Phone*
Address		
City & State	*Zip*	*Birthday*

Name		*Phone*
Address		
City & State	*Zip*	*Birthday*

Name		*Phone*
Address		
City & State	*Zip*	*Birthday*

Name		*Phone*
Address		
City & State	*Zip*	*Birthday*

Name		*Phone*
Address		
City & State	*Zip*	*Birthday*

Name		*Phone*
Address		
City & State	*Zip*	*Birthday*

Name		*Phone*
Address		
City & State	*Zip*	*Birthday*

Name		*Phone*
Address		
City & State	*Zip*	*Birthday*

Name		*Phone*
Address		
City & State	*Zip*	*Birthday*

Name		*Phone*
Address		
City & State	*Zip*	*Birthday*

Name		*Phone*
Address		
City & State	*Zip*	*Birthday*

Name		*Phone*
Address		
City & State	*Zip*	*Birthday*

Name		*Phone*
Address		
City & State	*Zip*	*Birthday*

Name		*Phone*
Address		
City & State	*Zip*	*Birthday*

Name		*Phone*
Address		
City & State	*Zip*	*Birthday*

Name		*Phone*
Address		
City & State	*Zip*	*Birthday*

BABY BLUE EYES (Nemophila menziesii), California.
Photograph by Jeff Foott/DRK Photo.

*The genus name of baby blue eyes (**Nemophila**) means "glade-loving" in Greek. These minute plants thrive in moist, shady forests from the coastal ranges of California and Oregon to the foothills of the Sierra Nevada. The fragile-looking flowers bloom from February to June.*

CLAMSHELL ORCHID (Epidendrum cochleatum), Florida.
Photograph by Larry West.

The genus name for this orchid means "upon a tree"—clamshell orchids grow on trees in swamps and woods in southern Florida. These epiphytes or air plants get their nutrients from the air and tree surfaces. A tropical species, this orchid also grows in Central and South America and the West Indies. Flowers appear from October to July.

Name _____   *Phone* _____

Address _____

City & State _____ *Zip* _____   *Birthday* _____

Name _____   *Phone* _____

Address _____

City & State _____ *Zip* _____   *Birthday* _____

Name _____   *Phone* _____

Address _____

City & State _____ *Zip* _____   *Birthday* _____

Name _____   *Phone* _____

Address _____

City & State _____ *Zip* _____   *Birthday* _____

Name _____   *Phone* _____

Address _____

City & State _____ *Zip* _____   *Birthday* _____

Name _____   *Phone* _____

Address _____

City & State _____ *Zip* _____   *Birthday* _____

Name _____   *Phone* _____

Address _____

City & State _____ *Zip* _____   *Birthday* _____

Name _____   *Phone* _____

Address _____

City & State _____ *Zip* _____   *Birthday* _____

Name	Phone
Address	
City & State	Zip	Birthday

Name	Phone
Address	
City & State	Zip	Birthday

Name	Phone
Address	
City & State	Zip	Birthday

Name	Phone
Address	
City & State	Zip	Birthday

Name	Phone
Address	
City & State	Zip	Birthday

Name	Phone
Address	
City & State	Zip	Birthday

Name	Phone
Address	
City & State	Zip	Birthday

Name	Phone
Address	
City & State	Zip	Birthday

Name _____ *Phone* _____

Address _____

City & State _____ *Zip* _____ *Birthday* _____

Name _____ *Phone* _____

Address _____

City & State _____ *Zip* _____ *Birthday* _____

Name _____ *Phone* _____

Address _____

City & State _____ *Zip* _____ *Birthday* _____

Name _____ *Phone* _____

Address _____

City & State _____ *Zip* _____ *Birthday* _____

Name _____ *Phone* _____

Address _____

City & State _____ *Zip* _____ *Birthday* _____

Name _____ *Phone* _____

Address _____

City & State _____ *Zip* _____ *Birthday* _____

Name _____ *Phone* _____

Address _____

City & State _____ *Zip* _____ *Birthday* _____

Name _____ *Phone* _____

Address _____

City & State _____ *Zip* _____ *Birthday* _____

Name _____ *Phone* _____

Address _____

City & State _____ *Zip* _____ *Birthday* _____

Name _____ *Phone* _____

Address _____

City & State _____ *Zip* _____ *Birthday* _____

Name _____ *Phone* _____

Address _____

City & State _____ *Zip* _____ *Birthday* _____

Name _____ *Phone* _____

Address _____

City & State _____ *Zip* _____ *Birthday* _____

Name _____ *Phone* _____

Address _____

City & State _____ *Zip* _____ *Birthday* _____

Name _____ *Phone* _____

Address _____

City & State _____ *Zip* _____ *Birthday* _____

Name _____ *Phone* _____

Address _____

City & State _____ *Zip* _____ *Birthday* _____

Name _____ *Phone* _____

Address _____

City & State _____ *Zip* _____ *Birthday* _____

BALSAMROOT (Balsamorhiza sp.), Oregon.
Photograph by Steve Terrill.

These robust members of the daisy family thrive on rocky slopes from the Sierra Nevada to the western Cascades, north to Canada, and east into the Rocky Mountains. The genus name, which means balsam root, refers to the aromatic taproot of those species. The flowers bloom from spring to summer.

GLOBEMALLOW (Sphaeralcea sp.), and ENGELMANN'S PRICKLY PEAR
(Opuntia engelmannii), Arizona.
Photograph by Larry Ulrich.

Found along roadsides, mesas, and sandy desert flats, globemallows range from southern California to Texas and south to Mexico. The orange flowers bloom from early spring to summer. Engelmann's prickly pear occurs in dry, sandy soils above 1,000 feet from Texas to Arizona and Mexico.

Name _____ *Phone* _____

Address _____

City & State _____ *Zip* ____ *Birthday* _____

Name _____ *Phone* _____

Address _____

City & State _____ *Zip* ____ *Birthday* _____

Name _____ *Phone* _____

Address _____

City & State _____ *Zip* ____ *Birthday* _____

Name _____ *Phone* _____

Address _____

City & State _____ *Zip* ____ *Birthday* _____

Name _____ *Phone* _____

Address _____

City & State _____ *Zip* ____ *Birthday* _____

Name _____ *Phone* _____

Address _____

City & State _____ *Zip* ____ *Birthday* _____

Name _____ *Phone* _____

Address _____

City & State _____ *Zip* ____ *Birthday* _____

Name _____ *Phone* _____

Address _____

City & State _____ *Zip* ____ *Birthday* _____

Name	*Phone*
Address	
City & State *Zip*	*Birthday*
Name	*Phone*
Address	
City & State *Zip*	*Birthday*
Name	*Phone*
Address	
City & State *Zip*	*Birthday*
Name	*Phone*
Address	
City & State *Zip*	*Birthday*
Name	*Phone*
Address	
City & State *Zip*	*Birthday*
Name	*Phone*
Address	
City & State *Zip*	*Birthday*
Name	*Phone*
Address	
City & State *Zip*	*Birthday*
Name	*Phone*
Address	
City & State *Zip*	*Birthday*

Name _____ *Phone* _____

Address _____

City & State _____ *Zip* ____ *Birthday* _____

Name _____ *Phone* _____

Address _____

City & State _____ *Zip* ____ *Birthday* _____

Name _____ *Phone* _____

Address _____

City & State _____ *Zip* ____ *Birthday* _____

Name _____ *Phone* _____

Address _____

City & State _____ *Zip* ____ *Birthday* _____

Name _____ *Phone* _____

Address _____

City & State _____ *Zip* ____ *Birthday* _____

Name _____ *Phone* _____

Address _____

City & State _____ *Zip* ____ *Birthday* _____

Name _____ *Phone* _____

Address _____

City & State _____ *Zip* ____ *Birthday* _____

Name _____ *Phone* _____

Address _____

City & State _____ *Zip* ____ *Birthday* _____

Name _____ *Phone* _____

Address _____

City & State _____ *Zip* _____ *Birthday* _____

Name _____ *Phone* _____

Address _____

City & State _____ *Zip* _____ *Birthday* _____

Name _____ *Phone* _____

Address _____

City & State _____ *Zip* _____ *Birthday* _____

Name _____ *Phone* _____

Address _____

City & State _____ *Zip* _____ *Birthday* _____

Name _____ *Phone* _____

Address _____

City & State _____ *Zip* _____ *Birthday* _____

Name _____ *Phone* _____

Address _____

City & State _____ *Zip* _____ *Birthday* _____

Name _____ *Phone* _____

Address _____

City & State _____ *Zip* _____ *Birthday* _____

Name _____ *Phone* _____

Address _____

City & State _____ *Zip* _____ *Birthday* _____

ALASKA BLUE ANEMONE (Anemone multiceps), Alaska.
Photograph by Stephen Krasemann/DRK Photo.

This delicate alpine anemone grows on rocky ledges, slopes, and forests in mountain ranges from northern California to Alaska and east to the Rocky Mountains. Covered with rough hairs, the blooms appear in early spring. Also called windflowers, anemones (from the Greek word for wind) disperse their seed by means of fluffy parachutes that catch the wind. The species name, which describes the leaves, means "many clefts."

ALPINE ASTERS (Aster sp.), Colorado.
Photograph by David Muench.

Several species of **Aster** *(and similar-looking members of the daisy family) occur in alpine zones of western and northwestern mountain ranges, often forming rounded mats. The flowers, which vary in color from pink to blue to white, bloom from July to August.*

Name		Phone
Address		
City & State	Zip	Birthday

Name		Phone
Address		
City & State	Zip	Birthday

Name		Phone
Address		
City & State	Zip	Birthday

*I*_J

Name		Phone
Address		
City & State	Zip	Birthday

Name		Phone
Address		
City & State	Zip	Birthday

Name		Phone
Address		
City & State	Zip	Birthday

Name		Phone
Address		
City & State	Zip	Birthday

Name		Phone
Address		
City & State	Zip	Birthday

Name _____ Phone _____

Address _____ _____

City & State _____ Zip _____ Birthday _____

Name _____ Phone _____

Address _____ _____

City & State _____ Zip _____ Birthday _____

Name _____ Phone _____

Address _____ _____

City & State _____ Zip _____ Birthday _____

Name _____ Phone _____

Address _____ _____

City & State _____ Zip _____ Birthday _____

Name _____ Phone _____

Address _____ _____

City & State _____ Zip _____ Birthday _____

Name _____ Phone _____

Address _____ _____

City & State _____ Zip _____ Birthday _____

Name _____ Phone _____

Address _____ _____

City & State _____ Zip _____ Birthday _____

Name _____ Phone _____

Address _____ _____

City & State _____ Zip _____ Birthday _____

Name	*Phone*
Address	
City & State *Zip*	*Birthday*

Name	*Phone*
Address	
City & State *Zip*	*Birthday*

Name	*Phone*
Address	
City & State *Zip*	*Birthday*

Name	*Phone*
Address	
City & State *Zip*	*Birthday*

Name	*Phone*
Address	
City & State *Zip*	*Birthday*

Name	*Phone*
Address	
City & State *Zip*	*Birthday*

Name	*Phone*
Address	
City & State *Zip*	*Birthday*

Name	*Phone*
Address	
City & State *Zip*	*Birthday*

Name _____ *Phone* _____

Address _____

City & State _____ *Zip* _____ *Birthday* _____

Name _____ *Phone* _____

Address _____

City & State _____ *Zip* _____ *Birthday* _____

Name _____ *Phone* _____

Address _____

City & State _____ *Zip* _____ *Birthday* _____

Name _____ *Phone* _____

Address _____

City & State _____ *Zip* _____ *Birthday* _____

Name _____ *Phone* _____

Address _____

City & State _____ *Zip* _____ *Birthday* _____

Name _____ *Phone* _____

Address _____

City & State _____ *Zip* _____ *Birthday* _____

Name _____ *Phone* _____

Address _____

City & State _____ *Zip* _____ *Birthday* _____

Name _____ *Phone* _____

Address _____

City & State _____ *Zip* _____ *Birthday* _____

LARGE-FLOWERED TRILLIUM (*Trillium grandiflorum*), New York.
Photograph by Steve Terrill.

The large white flowers of this species often turn pink with age. Found in moist woods and on hillsides from the Great Lakes region, east to New England, and south along the Appalachians, large-flowered trillium blooms in early spring. Like many members of the lily family, trilliums grow slowly and cannot be propagated easily; this leads to collection from the wild, which depletes natural stands.

SHARP-LOBED HEPATICA (Hepatica acutiloba), Minnesota.
Photograph by Mike Magnuson.
Also called liverleaf, hepatica's mottled leaves, which resemble liver tissue, were thought to cure liver ailments. Hepatica grows in moist forests from Maine to Minnesota and south to Georgia, Alabama, and Missouri. The white or purple blooms appear from March to June.

Name _____ Phone _____

Address _____

City & State _____ Zip _____ Birthday _____

Name _____ Phone _____

Address _____

City & State _____ Zip _____ Birthday _____

Name _____ Phone _____

Address _____

City & State _____ Zip _____ Birthday _____

Name _____ Phone _____

Address _____

City & State _____ Zip _____ Birthday _____

K

Name _____ Phone _____

Address _____

City & State _____ Zip _____ Birthday _____

Name _____ Phone _____

Address _____

City & State _____ Zip _____ Birthday _____

Name _____ Phone _____

Address _____

City & State _____ Zip _____ Birthday _____

Name _____ Phone _____

Address _____

City & State _____ Zip _____ Birthday _____

Name _____ *Phone* _____

Address _____

City & State _____ *Zip* _____ *Birthday* _____

Name _____ *Phone* _____

Address _____

City & State _____ *Zip* _____ *Birthday* _____

Name _____ *Phone* _____

Address _____

City & State _____ *Zip* _____ *Birthday* _____

Name _____ *Phone* _____

Address _____

City & State _____ *Zip* _____ *Birthday* _____

Name _____ *Phone* _____

Address _____

City & State _____ *Zip* _____ *Birthday* _____

Name _____ *Phone* _____

Address _____

City & State _____ *Zip* _____ *Birthday* _____

Name _____ *Phone* _____

Address _____

City & State _____ *Zip* _____ *Birthday* _____

Name _____ *Phone* _____

Address _____

City & State _____ *Zip* _____ *Birthday* _____

Name	*Phone*
Address	
City & State *Zip*	*Birthday*

Name	*Phone*
Address	
City & State *Zip*	*Birthday*

Name	*Phone*
Address	
City & State *Zip*	*Birthday*

Name	*Phone*
Address	
City & State *Zip*	*Birthday*

Name	*Phone*
Address	
City & State *Zip*	*Birthday*

Name	*Phone*
Address	
City & State *Zip*	*Birthday*

Name	*Phone*
Address	
City & State *Zip*	*Birthday*

Name	*Phone*
Address	
City & State *Zip*	*Birthday*

Name _____ *Phone* _____

Address _____

City & State _____ *Zip* _____ *Birthday* _____

Name _____ *Phone* _____

Address _____

City & State _____ *Zip* _____ *Birthday* _____

Name _____ *Phone* _____

Address _____

City & State _____ *Zip* _____ *Birthday* _____

Name _____ *Phone* _____

Address _____

City & State _____ *Zip* _____ *Birthday* _____

Name _____ *Phone* _____

Address _____

City & State _____ *Zip* _____ *Birthday* _____

Name _____ *Phone* _____

Address _____

City & State _____ *Zip* _____ *Birthday* _____

Name _____ *Phone* _____

Address _____

City & State _____ *Zip* _____ *Birthday* _____

Name _____ *Phone* _____

Address _____

City & State _____ *Zip* _____ *Birthday* _____

INDIAN PAINTBRUSH (Castilleja sp.), Utah.
Photograph by Tom Till.

*Although found throughout the United States, **Castilleja** species are more common in open, rocky areas and mountain meadows in the West. Paintbrush's colorful "petals" are actually modified leaves called bracts; the inconspicuous, yellowish flowers are found at the base of each bract. Indian paintbrush blooms from spring to summer.*

DUTCHMAN'S BREECHES (*Dicentra cucullaria*), *Tennessee.*
Photograph by John Shaw.

The unusual shape of this flower prompted its common name—Dutchman's breeches. Pollinators must spread the flower's elongated spurs in order to reach the nectar. Dutchman's breeches grow in moist woods and shady ledges from Quebec to Manitoba and across the eastern United States. The blossoms appear from April to June.

Name	*Phone*
Address	
City & State *Zip*	*Birthday*

Name	*Phone*
Address	
City & State *Zip*	*Birthday*

Name	*Phone*
Address	
City & State *Zip*	*Birthday*

Name	*Phone*
Address	
City & State *Zip*	*Birthday*

L

Name	*Phone*
Address	
City & State *Zip*	*Birthday*

Name	*Phone*
Address	
City & State *Zip*	*Birthday*

Name	*Phone*
Address	
City & State *Zip*	*Birthday*

Name	*Phone*
Address	
City & State *Zip*	*Birthday*

Name	*Phone*
Address	
City & State *Zip*	*Birthday*

Name	*Phone*
Address	
City & State *Zip*	*Birthday*

Name	*Phone*
Address	
City & State *Zip*	*Birthday*

Name	*Phone*
Address	
City & State *Zip*	*Birthday*

Name	*Phone*
Address	
City & State *Zip*	*Birthday*

Name	*Phone*
Address	
City & State *Zip*	*Birthday*

Name	*Phone*
Address	
City & State *Zip*	*Birthday*

Name	*Phone*
Address	
City & State *Zip*	*Birthday*

Name	*Phone*
Address	
City & State *Zip*	*Birthday*
Name	*Phone*
Address	
City & State *Zip*	*Birthday*
Name	*Phone*
Address	
City & State *Zip*	*Birthday*
Name	*Phone*
Address	
City & State *Zip*	*Birthday*
Name	*Phone*
Address	
City & State *Zip*	*Birthday*
Name	*Phone*
Address	
City & State *Zip*	*Birthday*
Name	*Phone*
Address	
City & State *Zip*	*Birthday*
Name	*Phone*
Address	
City & State *Zip*	*Birthday*

Name _____   *Phone* _____

Address _____

City & State _____ *Zip* _____   *Birthday* _____

Name _____   *Phone* _____

Address _____

City & State _____ *Zip* _____   *Birthday* _____

Name _____   *Phone* _____

Address _____

City & State _____ *Zip* _____   *Birthday* _____

Name _____   *Phone* _____

Address _____

City & State _____ *Zip* _____   *Birthday* _____

Name _____   *Phone* _____

Address _____

City & State _____ *Zip* _____   *Birthday* _____

Name _____   *Phone* _____

Address _____

City & State _____ *Zip* _____   *Birthday* _____

Name _____   *Phone* _____

Address _____

City & State _____ *Zip* _____   *Birthday* _____

Name _____   *Phone* _____

Address _____

City & State _____ *Zip* _____   *Birthday* _____

WOOD LILY (Lilium philadelphicum), Michigan.
Photograph by Rod Planck.

Preferring dry woods and thickets, wood lily occurs from eastern Canada, south to New England and the Appalachians, and west to Nebraska. Coloration in this species varies geographically, becoming redder in the western part of its range. The flowers bloom from June to August.

ALPINE GARDEN, *Washington.*
Photograph by Pat O'Hara.

Although subjected to extreme conditions, alpine zones offer a unique diversity of plant life. Highly sensitive to disturbance, those plants usually have dwarfed, ground-hugging foliage and, by comparison, large flowers. The mounded forms of alpine plants, surrounded by colorful lichens and mosses, create a gardenlike setting.

Name _____   *Phone* _____

Address _____

City & State _____ *Zip* _____   *Birthday* _____

Name _____   *Phone* _____

Address _____

City & State _____ *Zip* _____   *Birthday* _____

Name _____   *Phone* _____

Address _____

City & State _____ *Zip* _____   *Birthday* _____

Name _____   *Phone* _____

Address _____

City & State _____ *Zip* _____   *Birthday* _____

Name _____   *Phone* _____   *M*

Address _____

City & State _____ *Zip* _____   *Birthday* _____

Name _____   *Phone* _____

Address _____

City & State _____ *Zip* _____   *Birthday* _____

Name _____   *Phone* _____

Address _____

City & State _____ *Zip* _____   *Birthday* _____

Name _____   *Phone* _____

Address _____

City & State _____ *Zip* _____   *Birthday* _____

Name		Phone
Address		
City & State	Zip	Birthday

Name		Phone
Address		
City & State	Zip	Birthday

Name		Phone
Address		
City & State	Zip	Birthday

Name		Phone
Address		
City & State	Zip	Birthday

Name		Phone
Address		
City & State	Zip	Birthday

Name		Phone
Address		
City & State	Zip	Birthday

Name		Phone
Address		
City & State	Zip	Birthday

Name		Phone
Address		
City & State	Zip	Birthday

Name _____ *Phone* _____

Address _____

City & State _____ *Zip* _____ *Birthday* _____

Name _____ *Phone* _____

Address _____

City & State _____ *Zip* _____ *Birthday* _____

Name _____ *Phone* _____

Address _____

City & State _____ *Zip* _____ *Birthday* _____

Name _____ *Phone* _____

Address _____

City & State _____ *Zip* _____ *Birthday* _____

Name _____ *Phone* _____

Address _____

City & State _____ *Zip* _____ *Birthday* _____

Name _____ *Phone* _____

Address _____

City & State _____ *Zip* _____ *Birthday* _____

Name _____ *Phone* _____

Address _____

City & State _____ *Zip* _____ *Birthday* _____

Name _____ *Phone* _____

Address _____

City & State _____ *Zip* _____ *Birthday* _____

Name   *Phone*

Address

City & State   *Zip*   *Birthday*

Name   *Phone*

Address

City & State   *Zip*   *Birthday*

Name   *Phone*

Address

City & State   *Zip*   *Birthday*

Name   *Phone*

Address

City & State   *Zip*   *Birthday*

Name   *Phone*

Address

City & State   *Zip*   *Birthday*

Name   *Phone*

Address

City & State   *Zip*   *Birthday*

Name   *Phone*

Address

City & State   *Zip*   *Birthday*

YELLOW PAINTBRUSH (Castilleja sp.), Idaho.
Photograph by Jeff Gnass.

This genus of over 150 species is found most abundantly in the western states. Members of the snapdragon family, paintbrushes grow on rocky slopes, meadows, and foothills and bloom from spring to summer. Paintbrush species are often difficult to distinguish and are sometimes confused with **Orthocarpus** *or owl's clover, a closely related genus. The genus name for paintbrush honors Domingo Castillejo, a Spanish botanist.*

BLUE COLUMBINE (Aquilegia caerulea), Colorado.
Photograph by David Muench.

A favorite of hikers, blue columbine grows in rocky soils of mountain slopes, aspen groves, and moist forests from 6,000 to 11,000 feet. It ranges from Idaho to southwestern Montana and south to Arizona and New Mexico. The blue color of the flowers varies by region, becoming almost all white in some locations.

Name _____ *Phone* _____

Address _____

City & State _____ *Zip* _____ *Birthday* _____

Name _____ *Phone* _____

Address _____

City & State _____ *Zip* _____ *Birthday* _____

Name _____ *Phone* _____

Address _____

City & State _____ *Zip* _____ *Birthday* _____

Name _____ *Phone* _____

Address _____

City & State _____ *Zip* _____ *Birthday* _____

Name _____ *Phone* _____

Address _____

City & State _____ *Zip* _____ *Birthday* _____   *N*

Name _____ *Phone* _____

Address _____

City & State _____ *Zip* _____ *Birthday* _____

Name _____ *Phone* _____

Address _____

City & State _____ *Zip* _____ *Birthday* _____

Name _____ *Phone* _____

Address _____

City & State _____ *Zip* _____ *Birthday* _____

Name _____   *Phone* _____

Address _____

City & State _____ *Zip* _____   *Birthday* _____

Name _____   *Phone* _____

Address _____

City & State _____ *Zip* _____   *Birthday* _____

Name _____   *Phone* _____

Address _____

City & State _____ *Zip* _____   *Birthday* _____

Name _____   *Phone* _____

Address _____

City & State _____ *Zip* _____   *Birthday* _____

Name _____   *Phone* _____

Address _____

City & State _____ *Zip* _____   *Birthday* _____

Name _____   *Phone* _____

Address _____

City & State _____ *Zip* _____   *Birthday* _____

Name _____   *Phone* _____

Address _____

City & State _____ *Zip* _____   *Birthday* _____

Name _____   *Phone* _____

Address _____

City & State _____ *Zip* _____   *Birthday* _____

Name		*Phone*
Address		
City & State	*Zip*	*Birthday*

Name		*Phone*
Address		
City & State	*Zip*	*Birthday*

Name		*Phone*
Address		
City & State	*Zip*	*Birthday*

Name		*Phone*
Address		
City & State	*Zip*	*Birthday*

Name		*Phone*
Address		
City & State	*Zip*	*Birthday*

Name		*Phone*
Address		
City & State	*Zip*	*Birthday*

Name		*Phone*
Address		
City & State	*Zip*	*Birthday*

Name		*Phone*
Address		
City & State	*Zip*	*Birthday*

Name	*Phone*
Address	
City & State *Zip*	*Birthday*
Name	*Phone*
Address	
City & State *Zip*	*Birthday*
Name	*Phone*
Address	
City & State *Zip*	*Birthday*
Name	*Phone*
Address	
City & State *Zip*	*Birthday*
Name	*Phone*
Address	
City & State *Zip*	*Birthday*
Name	*Phone*
Address	
City & State *Zip*	*Birthday*
Name	*Phone*
Address	
City & State *Zip*	*Birthday*
Name	*Phone*
Address	
City & State *Zip*	*Birthday*

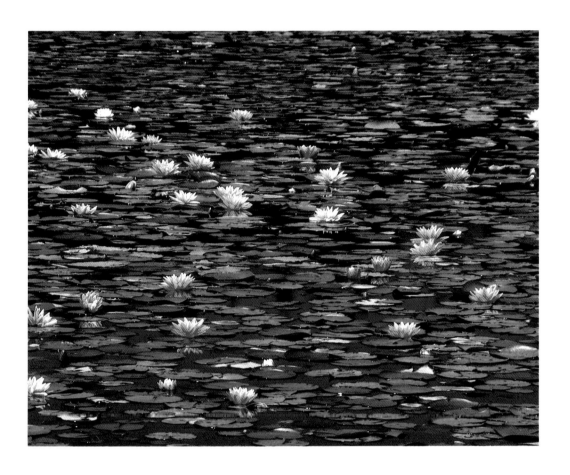

FRAGRANT WATER LILY (Nymphaea odorata), Maine.
Photograph by John Shaw.
Although water lilies appear to float freely in shallow ponds and lakes, these plants are actually firmly rooted. Their fragrant, showy blossoms, which appear from July to October, open only in the mornings. Native to the eastern states, fragrant water lily has expanded its range to quiet ponds and lakes throughout the United States.

YELLOW ROCK NETTLE (Eucnide bartonioides), *Texas.*
Photograph by Robert P. Carr.

A member of the loasa family, this succulent grows in dry soils of south Texas. Its rough leaves have stinging hairs. The flowers, which open only in bright sunshine, bloom from spring through fall.

Name _____ Phone _____

Address _____

City & State _____ Zip _____ Birthday _____

Name _____ Phone _____

Address _____

City & State _____ Zip _____ Birthday _____

Name _____ Phone _____

Address _____

City & State _____ Zip _____ Birthday _____

Name _____ Phone _____

Address _____

City & State _____ Zip _____ Birthday _____

Name _____ Phone _____

Address _____

City & State _____ Zip _____ Birthday _____

Name _____ Phone _____ O

Address _____

City & State _____ Zip _____ Birthday _____

Name _____ Phone _____

Address _____

City & State _____ Zip _____ Birthday _____

Name _____ Phone _____

Address _____

City & State _____ Zip _____ Birthday _____

Name _____   *Phone* _____

Address _____

City & State _____ *Zip* _____ *Birthday* _____

Name _____   *Phone* _____

Address _____

City & State _____ *Zip* _____ *Birthday* _____

Name _____   *Phone* _____

Address _____

City & State _____ *Zip* _____ *Birthday* _____

Name _____   *Phone* _____

Address _____

City & State _____ *Zip* _____ *Birthday* _____

Name _____   *Phone* _____

Address _____

City & State _____ *Zip* _____ *Birthday* _____

Name _____   *Phone* _____

Address _____

City & State _____ *Zip* _____ *Birthday* _____

Name _____   *Phone* _____

Address _____

City & State _____ *Zip* _____ *Birthday* _____

Name _____   *Phone* _____

Address _____

City & State _____ *Zip* _____ *Birthday* _____

Name		_Phone_
Address		
City & State	_Zip_	_Birthday_
Name		_Phone_
Address		
City & State	_Zip_	_Birthday_
Name		_Phone_
Address		
City & State	_Zip_	_Birthday_
Name		_Phone_
Address		
City & State	_Zip_	_Birthday_
Name		_Phone_
Address		
City & State	_Zip_	_Birthday_
Name		_Phone_
Address		
City & State	_Zip_	_Birthday_
Name		_Phone_
Address		
City & State	_Zip_	_Birthday_
Name		_Phone_
Address		
City & State	_Zip_	_Birthday_

Name _____   *Phone* _____

Address _____

City & State _____ *Zip* _____   *Birthday* _____

Name _____   *Phone* _____

Address _____

City & State _____ *Zip* _____   *Birthday* _____

Name _____   *Phone* _____

Address _____

City & State _____ *Zip* _____   *Birthday* _____

Name _____   *Phone* _____

Address _____

City & State _____ *Zip* _____   *Birthday* _____

Name _____   *Phone* _____

Address _____

City & State _____ *Zip* _____   *Birthday* _____

Name _____   *Phone* _____

Address _____

City & State _____ *Zip* _____   *Birthday* _____

Name _____   *Phone* _____

Address _____

City & State _____ *Zip* _____   *Birthday* _____

Name _____   *Phone* _____

Address _____

City & State _____ *Zip* _____   *Birthday* _____

LEWIS'S MONKEYFLOWER (Mimulus lewisii) and OAK FERNS
(Gymnocarpium sp.), Washington.
Photograph by John Shaw.

One of the showiest mountain wildflowers, Lewis's monkeyflower occurs in wet meadows and along
stream banks in subalpine and alpine zones. Blooming from June to August, this species ranges from
western Canada, south to the Sierra Nevada and the mountains of Utah, Wyoming, and Montana.

ASTERS (*Aster* sp.), Colorado.
Photograph by Steve Terrill.

A genus of several hundred species, **Aster** species are often difficult to distinguish due to their variability
and hybridization. The name **Aster**, derived from the Greek word for star, describes the starlike aspect
of the flower. Found widespread throughout the United States, asters bloom in late summer or early fall.

Name _____ Phone _____

Address _____

City & State _____ Zip _____ Birthday _____

Name _____ Phone _____

Address _____

City & State _____ Zip _____ Birthday _____

Name _____ Phone _____

Address _____

City & State _____ Zip _____ Birthday _____

Name _____ Phone _____

Address _____

City & State _____ Zip _____ Birthday _____

Name _____ Phone _____

Address _____

City & State _____ Zip _____ Birthday _____

Name _____ Phone _____

Address _____

City & State _____ Zip _____ Birthday _____

P

Name _____ Phone _____

Address _____

City & State _____ Zip _____ Birthday _____

Name _____ Phone _____

Address _____

City & State _____ Zip _____ Birthday _____

Name _____ *Phone* _____

Address _____

City & State _____ *Zip* _____ *Birthday* _____

Name _____ *Phone* _____

Address _____

City & State _____ *Zip* _____ *Birthday* _____

Name _____ *Phone* _____

Address _____

City & State _____ *Zip* _____ *Birthday* _____

Name _____ *Phone* _____

Address _____

City & State _____ *Zip* _____ *Birthday* _____

Name _____ *Phone* _____

Address _____

City & State _____ *Zip* _____ *Birthday* _____

Name _____ *Phone* _____

Address _____

City & State _____ *Zip* _____ *Birthday* _____

Name _____ *Phone* _____

Address _____

City & State _____ *Zip* _____ *Birthday* _____

Name _____ *Phone* _____

Address _____

City & State _____ *Zip* _____ *Birthday* _____

Name	*Phone*
Address	
City & State *Zip*	*Birthday*

Name	*Phone*
Address	
City & State *Zip*	*Birthday*

Name	*Phone*
Address	
City & State *Zip*	*Birthday*

Name	*Phone*
Address	
City & State *Zip*	*Birthday*

Name	*Phone*
Address	
City & State *Zip*	*Birthday*

Name	*Phone*
Address	
City & State *Zip*	*Birthday*

Name	*Phone*
Address	
City & State *Zip*	*Birthday*

Name	*Phone*
Address	
City & State *Zip*	*Birthday*

Name _____ *Phone* _____

Address _____

City & State _____ *Zip* _____ *Birthday* _____

Name _____ *Phone* _____

Address _____

City & State _____ *Zip* _____ *Birthday* _____

Name _____ *Phone* _____

Address _____

City & State _____ *Zip* _____ *Birthday* _____

Name _____ *Phone* _____

Address _____

City & State _____ *Zip* _____ *Birthday* _____

Name _____ *Phone* _____

Address _____

City & State _____ *Zip* _____ *Birthday* _____

Name _____ *Phone* _____

Address _____

City & State _____ *Zip* _____ *Birthday* _____

Name _____ *Phone* _____

Address _____

City & State _____ *Zip* _____ *Birthday* _____

Name _____ *Phone* _____

Address _____

City & State _____ *Zip* _____ *Birthday* _____

CALIFORNIA POPPY (Eschscholzia californica), California.
Photograph by Carr Clifton.
Found on open coastal hillsides in Oregon and northwest California, this poppy blooms from May to September. The genus name honors Dr. Johann F. Eschscholz, a surgeon and naturalist who participated in Russian expeditions to the United States in the early 1800s. The sap from California poppies reportedly was used by Native Americans to treat toothaches.

RABBITBRUSH (Chrysothamnus nauseosus), Oregon.
Photograph by Steve Terrill.

This shrublike plant is found on dry, sandy soils of plains and roadsides from Texas to California, north to Canada, and south to Mexico. Because rabbitbrush thrives in poor soils, it is a good indicator of areas that have been overgrazed or disturbed. A member of the daisy family, rabbitbrush blooms from mid-summer to fall.

Name _____ *Phone* _____

Address _____

City & State _____ *Zip* ___ *Birthday* _____

Name _____ *Phone* _____

Address _____

City & State _____ *Zip* ___ *Birthday* _____

Name _____ *Phone* _____

Address _____

City & State _____ *Zip* ___ *Birthday* _____

Name _____ *Phone* _____

Address _____

City & State _____ *Zip* ___ *Birthday* _____

Name _____ *Phone* _____

Address _____

City & State _____ *Zip* ___ *Birthday* _____

Name _____ *Phone* _____

Address _____

City & State _____ *Zip* ___ *Birthday* _____

Name _____ *Phone* _____

Address _____

City & State _____ *Zip* ___ *Birthday* _____

Name _____ *Phone* _____

Address _____

City & State _____ *Zip* ___ *Birthday* _____

Q_R

Name _____ *Phone* _____

Address _____

City & State _____ *Zip* _____ *Birthday* _____

Name _____ *Phone* _____

Address _____

City & State _____ *Zip* _____ *Birthday* _____

Name _____ *Phone* _____

Address _____

City & State _____ *Zip* _____ *Birthday* _____

Name _____ *Phone* _____

Address _____

City & State _____ *Zip* _____ *Birthday* _____

Name _____ *Phone* _____

Address _____

City & State _____ *Zip* _____ *Birthday* _____

Name _____ *Phone* _____

Address _____

City & State _____ *Zip* _____ *Birthday* _____

Name _____ *Phone* _____

Address _____

City & State _____ *Zip* _____ *Birthday* _____

Name _____ *Phone* _____

Address _____

City & State _____ *Zip* _____ *Birthday* _____

Name	*Phone*
Address	
City & State *Zip*	*Birthday*

Name	*Phone*
Address	
City & State *Zip*	*Birthday*

Name	*Phone*
Address	
City & State *Zip*	*Birthday*

Name	*Phone*
Address	
City & State *Zip*	*Birthday*

Name	*Phone*
Address	
City & State *Zip*	*Birthday*

Name	*Phone*
Address	
City & State *Zip*	*Birthday*

Name	*Phone*
Address	
City & State *Zip*	*Birthday*

Name	*Phone*
Address	
City & State *Zip*	*Birthday*

Name		*Phone*
Address		
City & State	*Zip*	*Birthday*

Name		*Phone*
Address		
City & State	*Zip*	*Birthday*

Name		*Phone*
Address		
City & State	*Zip*	*Birthday*

Name		*Phone*
Address		
City & State	*Zip*	*Birthday*

Name		*Phone*
Address		
City & State	*Zip*	*Birthday*

Name		*Phone*
Address		
City & State	*Zip*	*Birthday*

Name		*Phone*
Address		
City & State	*Zip*	*Birthday*

Name		*Phone*
Address		
City & State	*Zip*	*Birthday*

PURPLE-FRINGED ORCHID (Platanthera sp.), Michigan.
Photograph by Rod Planck.

Purple-fringed orchid grows in wet meadows, bogs, and moist woods from Newfoundland to New England, south to Tennessee, and west to Wisconsin. Its fragrant flowers, which bloom from June to August, are specially adapted for pollination by moths.

COLUMBINE *(Aquilegia sp.), Oregon.*
Photograph by Steve Terrill.

Columbines range throughout the United States, but are more common in the West. The plants, which prefer shady areas, moist meadows, and rocky slopes, bloom from spring to summer. The common name is derived from the Latin word for dove; the flowers were thought to look like hovering doves. Lion's herb is another name for columbine because, according to one myth, lions ate the plant for strength.

Name _____   *Phone* _____

Address _____

City & State _____ *Zip* _____   *Birthday* _____

Name _____   *Phone* _____

Address _____

City & State _____ *Zip* _____   *Birthday* _____

Name _____   *Phone* _____

Address _____

City & State _____ *Zip* _____   *Birthday* _____

Name _____   *Phone* _____

Address _____

City & State _____ *Zip* _____   *Birthday* _____

Name _____   *Phone* _____

Address _____

City & State _____ *Zip* _____   *Birthday* _____

Name _____   *Phone* _____

Address _____

City & State _____ *Zip* _____   *Birthday* _____

Name _____   *Phone* _____

Address _____

City & State _____ *Zip* _____   *Birthday* _____

S

Name _____   *Phone* _____

Address _____

City & State _____ *Zip* _____   *Birthday* _____

Name _____   *Phone* _____

Address _____

City & State _____ *Zip* _____   *Birthday* _____

Name _____   *Phone* _____

Address _____

City & State _____ *Zip* _____   *Birthday* _____

Name _____   *Phone* _____

Address _____

City & State _____ *Zip* _____   *Birthday* _____

Name _____   *Phone* _____

Address _____

City & State _____ *Zip* _____   *Birthday* _____

Name _____   *Phone* _____

Address _____

City & State _____ *Zip* _____   *Birthday* _____

Name _____   *Phone* _____

Address _____

City & State _____ *Zip* _____   *Birthday* _____

Name _____   *Phone* _____

Address _____

City & State _____ *Zip* _____   *Birthday* _____

Name _____   *Phone* _____

Address _____

City & State _____ *Zip* _____   *Birthday* _____

Name		Phone	
Address			
City & State	Zip	Birthday	

Name		Phone	
Address			
City & State	Zip	Birthday	

Name		Phone	
Address			
City & State	Zip	Birthday	

Name		Phone	
Address			
City & State	Zip	Birthday	

Name		Phone	
Address			
City & State	Zip	Birthday	

Name		Phone	
Address			
City & State	Zip	Birthday	

Name		Phone	
Address			
City & State	Zip	Birthday	

Name		Phone	
Address			
City & State	Zip	Birthday	

Name _____ *Phone* _____

Address _____

City & State _____ *Zip* _____ *Birthday* _____

Name _____ *Phone* _____

Address _____

City & State _____ *Zip* _____ *Birthday* _____

Name _____ *Phone* _____

Address _____

City & State _____ *Zip* _____ *Birthday* _____

Name _____ *Phone* _____

Address _____

City & State _____ *Zip* _____ *Birthday* _____

Name _____ *Phone* _____

Address _____

City & State _____ *Zip* _____ *Birthday* _____

Name _____ *Phone* _____

Address _____

City & State _____ *Zip* _____ *Birthday* _____

Name _____ *Phone* _____

Address _____

City & State _____ *Zip* _____ *Birthday* _____

Name _____ *Phone* _____

Address _____

City & State _____ *Zip* _____ *Birthday* _____

MEXICAN POPPIES *(Eschscholzia mexicana)*, LUPINE *(Lupinus sp.)*, and BRITTLEBUSH
(Encelia farinosa), Arizona.
Photograph by Mike Magnuson.

Desert wildflowers such as poppies and lupines take advantage of spring rains, often carpeting large open areas with their contrasting colors. Well-adapted to hot dry deserts, brittlebush spends most of the year in a shriveled, moisture-conserving state, until sufficient moisture induces it to produce larger, green leaves and mounds of yellow blossoms.

BUTTER-AND-EGGS (Linaria vulgaris), New York.
Photograph by J.F. Martin.

Also called toadflax, butter-and-eggs has become naturalized over much of the United States.
Originally from Eurasia, butter-and-eggs thrives in disturbed areas and along roadsides. The flowers,
which have a strong, rather rank odor, bloom from June to September.

Name _____ Phone _____

Address _____

City & State _____ Zip _____ Birthday _____

Name _____ Phone _____

Address _____

City & State _____ Zip _____ Birthday _____

Name _____ Phone _____

Address _____

City & State _____ Zip _____ Birthday _____

Name _____ Phone _____

Address _____

City & State _____ Zip _____ Birthday _____

Name _____ Phone _____

Address _____

City & State _____ Zip _____ Birthday _____

Name _____ Phone _____

Address _____

City & State _____ Zip _____ Birthday _____

Name _____ Phone _____

Address _____

City & State _____ Zip _____ Birthday _____

Name _____ Phone _____

Address _____

City & State _____ Zip _____ Birthday _____

T

Name	*Phone*
Address	
City & State *Zip*	*Birthday*
Name	*Phone*
Address	
City & State *Zip*	*Birthday*
Name	*Phone*
Address	
City & State *Zip*	*Birthday*
Name	*Phone*
Address	
City & State *Zip*	*Birthday*
Name	*Phone*
Address	
City & State *Zip*	*Birthday*
Name	*Phone*
Address	
City & State *Zip*	*Birthday*
Name	*Phone*
Address	
City & State *Zip*	*Birthday*
Name	*Phone*
Address	
City & State *Zip*	*Birthday*

Name		*Phone*
Address		
City & State	*Zip*	*Birthday*
Name		*Phone*
Address		
City & State	*Zip*	*Birthday*
Name		*Phone*
Address		
City & State	*Zip*	*Birthday*
Name		*Phone*
Address		
City & State	*Zip*	*Birthday*
Name		*Phone*
Address		
City & State	*Zip*	*Birthday*
Name		*Phone*
Address		
City & State	*Zip*	*Birthday*
Name		*Phone*
Address		
City & State	*Zip*	*Birthday*
Name		*Phone*
Address		
City & State	*Zip*	*Birthday*

Name _____   *Phone* _____

Address _____

City & State _____ *Zip* _____   *Birthday* _____

Name _____   *Phone* _____

Address _____

City & State _____ *Zip* _____   *Birthday* _____

Name _____   *Phone* _____

Address _____

City & State _____ *Zip* _____   *Birthday* _____

Name _____   *Phone* _____

Address _____

City & State _____ *Zip* _____   *Birthday* _____

Name _____   *Phone* _____

Address _____

City & State _____ *Zip* _____   *Birthday* _____

Name _____   *Phone* _____

Address _____

City & State _____ *Zip* _____   *Birthday* _____

Name _____   *Phone* _____

Address _____

City & State _____ *Zip* _____   *Birthday* _____

Name _____   *Phone* _____

Address _____

City & State _____ *Zip* _____   *Birthday* _____

PINK EVENING PRIMROSE (Oenothera speciosa), Texas.
Photograph by David Muench.

Found in fields, prairies, and roadsides from Missouri to Kansas and south to Texas and Mexico, pink evening primrose blooms from May to July. Although this species usually opens during the day, many species in the evening primrose family flower at dusk—their pale blooms attract night pollinators, such as moths. The National Wildflower Research Center has chosen this lovely spring wildflower for its logo.

DAISIES (Chrysanthemum sp.), New Jersey.
Photograph by Tom Till.

Introduced from Europe, daisies have become naturalized and occur throughout the United States. Found in fields, disturbed areas, and along roadsides, the flowers bloom from May to October. The name daisy is derived from Anglo-Saxon words meaning "day's eye." The flower was thought to look like the sun—the eye of the day.

Name _____ Phone _____

Address _____

City & State _____ Zip _____ Birthday _____

Name _____ Phone _____

Address _____

City & State _____ Zip _____ Birthday _____

Name _____ Phone _____

Address _____

City & State _____ Zip _____ Birthday _____

Name _____ Phone _____

Address _____

City & State _____ Zip _____ Birthday _____

Name _____ Phone _____

Address _____

City & State _____ Zip _____ Birthday _____

Name _____ Phone _____

Address _____

City & State _____ Zip _____ Birthday _____

Name _____ Phone _____

Address _____

City & State _____ Zip _____ Birthday _____

Name _____ Phone _____

Address _____

City & State _____ Zip _____ Birthday _____

U
V

Name		*Phone*
Address		
City & State	*Zip*	*Birthday*

Name		*Phone*
Address		
City & State	*Zip*	*Birthday*

Name		*Phone*
Address		
City & State	*Zip*	*Birthday*

Name		*Phone*
Address		
City & State	*Zip*	*Birthday*

Name		*Phone*
Address		
City & State	*Zip*	*Birthday*

Name		*Phone*
Address		
City & State	*Zip*	*Birthday*

Name		*Phone*
Address		
City & State	*Zip*	*Birthday*

Name		*Phone*
Address		
City & State	*Zip*	*Birthday*

Name		*Phone*
Address		
City & State	*Zip*	*Birthday*

Name		*Phone*
Address		
City & State	*Zip*	*Birthday*

Name		*Phone*
Address		
City & State	*Zip*	*Birthday*

Name		*Phone*
Address		
City & State	*Zip*	*Birthday*

Name		*Phone*
Address		
City & State	*Zip*	*Birthday*

Name		*Phone*
Address		
City & State	*Zip*	*Birthday*

Name		*Phone*
Address		
City & State	*Zip*	*Birthday*

Name		*Phone*
Address		
City & State	*Zip*	*Birthday*

Name	*Phone*
Address	
City & State　　　　　*Zip*	*Birthday*
Name	*Phone*
Address	
City & State　　　　　*Zip*	*Birthday*
Name	*Phone*
Address	
City & State　　　　　*Zip*	*Birthday*
Name	*Phone*
Address	
City & State　　　　　*Zip*	*Birthday*
Name	*Phone*
Address	
City & State　　　　　*Zip*	*Birthday*
Name	*Phone*
Address	
City & State　　　　　*Zip*	*Birthday*
Name	*Phone*
Address	
City & State　　　　　*Zip*	*Birthday*
Name	*Phone*
Address	
City & State　　　　　*Zip*	*Birthday*

WESTERN AZALEAS *(Rhododendron occidentale), California.*
Photograph by Larry Ulrich.

The showy two-toned blossoms of western azaleas add color to shady stream banks and moist areas
below 7,500 feet. Ranging from northern California to Oregon, the flowers bloom from April to August.

TREE LUPINES (Lupinus arboreus), California.
Photograph by Larry Ulrich.

Though tree lupines are primarily shrublike in form, they can reach heights of nine feet. Native to the sandy soils of California coasts, tree lupines are often planted for erosion control in coastal areas. The yellow (or occasionally blue) flowers bloom from March to September.

Name _____ Phone _____

Address _____

City & State _____ Zip _____ Birthday _____

Name _____ Phone _____

Address _____

City & State _____ Zip _____ Birthday _____

Name _____ Phone _____

Address _____

City & State _____ Zip _____ Birthday _____

Name _____ Phone _____

Address _____

City & State _____ Zip _____ Birthday _____

Name _____ Phone _____

Address _____

City & State _____ Zip _____ Birthday _____

Name _____ Phone _____

Address _____

City & State _____ Zip _____ Birthday _____

Name _____ Phone _____

Address _____

City & State _____ Zip _____ Birthday _____

Name _____ Phone _____

Address _____

City & State _____ Zip _____ Birthday _____

W

Name		Phone	
Address			
City & State	Zip	Birthday	

Name		Phone	
Address			
City & State	Zip	Birthday	

Name		Phone	
Address			
City & State	Zip	Birthday	

Name		Phone	
Address			
City & State	Zip	Birthday	

Name		Phone	
Address			
City & State	Zip	Birthday	

Name		Phone	
Address			
City & State	Zip	Birthday	

Name		Phone	
Address			
City & State	Zip	Birthday	

Name		Phone	
Address			
City & State	Zip	Birthday	

Name		*Phone*
Address		
City & State	*Zip*	*Birthday*

Name		*Phone*
Address		
City & State	*Zip*	*Birthday*

Name		*Phone*
Address		
City & State	*Zip*	*Birthday*

Name		*Phone*
Address		
City & State	*Zip*	*Birthday*

Name		*Phone*
Address		
City & State	*Zip*	*Birthday*

Name		*Phone*
Address		
City & State	*Zip*	*Birthday*

Name		*Phone*
Address		
City & State	*Zip*	*Birthday*

Name		*Phone*
Address		
City & State	*Zip*	*Birthday*

Name _____ *Phone* _____

Address _____

City & State _____ *Zip* _____ *Birthday* _____

Name _____ *Phone* _____

Address _____

City & State _____ *Zip* _____ *Birthday* _____

Name _____ *Phone* _____

Address _____

City & State _____ *Zip* _____ *Birthday* _____

Name _____ *Phone* _____

Address _____

City & State _____ *Zip* _____ *Birthday* _____

Name _____ *Phone* _____

Address _____

City & State _____ *Zip* _____ *Birthday* _____

Name _____ *Phone* _____

Address _____

City & State _____ *Zip* _____ *Birthday* _____

Name _____ *Phone* _____

Address _____

City & State _____ *Zip* _____ *Birthday* _____

Name _____ *Phone* _____

Address _____

City & State _____ *Zip* _____ *Birthday* _____

NORTHERN BLAZING STAR (*Liatris borealis*), *Michigan.*
Photograph by John Gerlach/DRK Photo.

A prairie plant of dry open woods and thickets, northern blazing star ranges from Maine to Michigan and south to Pennsylvania, West Virginia, and Arkansas. The purplish flower stalks, which bloom in late summer or early fall, provide food for migrating butterflies and other insects.

SHEEP LAUREL *(Kalmia angustifolia)* and BLACK SPRUCE *(Picea mariana)*, *Michigan.*
Photograph by Rod Planck.

An evergreen shrub, sheep laurel occurs in dry to wet sandy soils of oil fields and bogs. Named for Peter Kalm, a student of the Swedish botanist Linnaeus, sheep laurel ranges from Manitoba to Newfoundland, south to the Appalachians, and west to Michigan. The bell-like flowers bloom from May to August.

Name _____ *Phone* _____

Address _____

City & State _____ *Zip* _____ *Birthday* _____

Name _____ *Phone* _____

Address _____

City & State _____ *Zip* _____ *Birthday* _____

Name _____ *Phone* _____

Address _____

City & State _____ *Zip* _____ *Birthday* _____

Name _____ *Phone* _____

Address _____

City & State _____ *Zip* _____ *Birthday* _____

Name _____ *Phone* _____

Address _____

City & State _____ *Zip* _____ *Birthday* _____

Name _____ *Phone* _____

Address _____

City & State _____ *Zip* _____ *Birthday* _____

Name _____ *Phone* _____

Address _____

City & State _____ *Zip* _____ *Birthday* _____

Name _____ *Phone* _____

Address _____

City & State _____ *Zip* _____ *Birthday* _____

X Y Z

Name		*Phone*
Address		
City & State	*Zip*	*Birthday*

Name		*Phone*
Address		
City & State	*Zip*	*Birthday*

Name		*Phone*
Address		
City & State	*Zip*	*Birthday*

Name		*Phone*
Address		
City & State	*Zip*	*Birthday*

Name		*Phone*
Address		
City & State	*Zip*	*Birthday*

Name		*Phone*
Address		
City & State	*Zip*	*Birthday*

Name		*Phone*
Address		
City & State	*Zip*	*Birthday*

Name		*Phone*
Address		
City & State	*Zip*	*Birthday*

Name _____ Phone _____

Address _____

City & State _____ Zip _____ Birthday _____

Name _____ Phone _____

Address _____

City & State _____ Zip _____ Birthday _____

Name _____ Phone _____

Address _____

City & State _____ Zip _____ Birthday _____

Name _____ Phone _____

Address _____

City & State _____ Zip _____ Birthday _____

Name _____ Phone _____

Address _____

City & State _____ Zip _____ Birthday _____

Name _____ Phone _____

Address _____

City & State _____ Zip _____ Birthday _____

Name _____ Phone _____

Address _____

City & State _____ Zip _____ Birthday _____

Name _____ Phone _____

Address _____

City & State _____ Zip _____ Birthday _____

Name _____   *Phone* _____

Address _____

City & State _____ *Zip* _____   *Birthday* _____

Name _____   *Phone* _____

Address _____

City & State _____ *Zip* _____   *Birthday* _____

Name _____   *Phone* _____

Address _____

City & State _____ *Zip* _____   *Birthday* _____

Name _____   *Phone* _____

Address _____

City & State _____ *Zip* _____   *Birthday* _____

Name _____   *Phone* _____

Address _____

City & State _____ *Zip* _____   *Birthday* _____

Name _____   *Phone* _____

Address _____

City & State _____ *Zip* _____   *Birthday* _____

Name _____   *Phone* _____

Address _____

City & State _____ *Zip* _____   *Birthday* _____

Name _____   *Phone* _____

Address _____

City & State _____ *Zip* _____   *Birthday* _____